JESSICA A. WILEY

Recognizing

RED
FLAGS

A Single Woman's Guide to Identifying
Toxic Warning Signs While Dating

ENTEGRITY
CHOICE PUBLISHING

All scriptures are from the King James Version
of the bible unless otherwise noted.

Entegrity Choice Publishing
PO Box 453
Powder Springs, GA 30127
info@entegritypublishing.com
www.entegritypublishing.com
404.472.9190

Printed in the United States of America

Library of Congress Cataloging-in-Publication Data
ISBN 979-8-9991668-1-4
Library of Congress Control Number: 2025917732

To my mother and father, whose love and respect have been my greatest examples. Through their stories, guidance, and openness, I'm growing into a better woman with each passing day.

CONTENTS

PAY ATTENTION TO
HOW A MAN TREATS YOU

*"When you meet a man and
see a red flag, do not ignore it."*

Is he kind, or does he have a temper?

Does he monopolize conversations, or
does he welcome healthy exchanges?

Is he concerned about you, or is he self-serving?

PREFACE

Recognizing Red Flags: A Single Woman's Guide to Identifying Toxic Warning Signs While Dating gives singles an inside look on what to pay attention to while dating. This body of work is direct, specific, and most definitely a conversation piece. This book is for women who did not get the memo on warning signs that deserved their attention during the dating process, or they have simply decided to ignore the signs that appear in an unhealthy relationship. Whether singles are in a short-term or long-term relationship, this book will help them identify any red flags.

A red flag is a metaphor to indicate a particular problem or signal danger. I believe some women are either uneducated about what healthy dating should look like, or they have decided to accept toxic behaviors because they have become desperate for companionship.

When women do not recognize red flags, it leaves room for confusion, heartbreak, and even the possibility of not being open to receiving true love in the future. My goal in authoring this book is to equip singles not only to identify red flags while dating but also to take ownership of their mistakes and remember how valuable they are. I have experienced every one of the observation points highlighted throughout this book while dating. I am confident that once you have read this informative book, you will have the skill set to begin a fresh, new, healthy approach to dating, enjoy the process, and be aware of red flags that may present themselves.

YOUR INTUITION
IS RARELY
INCORRECT

Intuition means the ability to understand something immediately without the need for conscious reasoning. Have you ever had an unexplainable feeling while dating? Did you acknowledge it or ignore it? Paying attention to your intuition could save you loads of headaches and heartaches.

Take it slowly.

Watch closely and listen attentively.

Doing this gives you the advantage.

You can then choose whether you would like to proceed with entertaining your date.

2

PAY ATTENTION
TO WHAT YOU SEE

Have you ever read a book and wanted to insert a word that is not there? While rereading, you realize you added your own words.

This is what we do in relationships.

We see what we want to see.

I have heard stories of women who have survived abusive relationships. They said they knew something was wrong at the beginning of the relationship. Some said there were indicators early in the relationship that they ignored. Imagine the trauma they could have avoided if they acknowledged their female intuition.

3

WHILE DATING,
TAKE IT SLOWLY

It is okay to talk and get to know each other. Where is the fire? Why rush? Dating gives you an opportunity to collect data about the other person.

Acknowledging what you have learned will allow you to determine if you are genuinely interested in developing a relationship.

Unfortunately, some people move at an accelerated pace and leave no room for conversation that should lead to learning about each other. This is a red flag. Slowing things down is both an option and your right. I do not know about other people, but when a guy is pushing me to move super-fast, I start to wonder why and ask myself whether he behaves like this with other women. It can prove to be extremely unsafe as well as careless.

Ladies, know that pressure should never be the order of the day. Take your time. It is in your best interest to move at a healthy pace.

INTELLECTUAL
BALANCE

*"Date people who match
your intellectual level."*

You do not have to go for the underdog.

Stand firm in visualizing the type of man you want to be with. Choosing whether to entertain a man is your decision. It is no different from selecting furniture or friends. Look at what is being presented and select the one that best fits your needs and desires.

For example, you would not select furniture that would not support your weight. You would look for something sturdy and of quality construction. The same applies when you are choosing a mate. Make sure his conversation holds your interest.

Do not feel bad if you choose not to remain in a relationship with someone who does not ignite you intellectually.

LOVE VERSUS THINGS

"Solely being showered with flowers or gifts does not mean a man loves you."

Unfortunately, some people equate love with material items, alone. They feel a man does not love them if he is not loading them with Gucci, Louis Vuitton or Tiffany & Company. This is a superficial mind frame and one that is not a true barometer on love.

Love is not based on how much money a man spends on a woman. The manifestation of a man's love is based on how he treats you. Ask yourself if he is available when it matters. Is he engaged in your life, aspirations and goals? Does he ever ask how your child or children are doing? This is a short-list of what really matters.

Gifts are a bonus and you should be appreciative. However things are not the determining factor in whether or not a man truly loves you. A man's loyalty and faithfulness to you, his availability (mentally, emotionally and financially), his concern for you and your children are what matters the most.

Instead of focusing on material things ask yourself does he do what needs to be done without you asking? Are you at peace when you are together? These are relevant questions. The answers to these questions will determine if a man truly loves you or not.

6

CONSEQUENCES FOLLOW DESPERATION

When relationships are not progressing rapidly enough for us, we can get sloppy. We transition from patiently waiting for our "person" to forcing ourselves to remain in unhealthy relationships. Revealing that we have officially entered a place of desperation.

The problem with becoming desperate is that it causes you to do *anything* you can to get the thing you have been hoping for and waiting for. The sad part is consequences are the by-product of desperation. For some women, they built a relationship with someone they are unhappy with, and now they are having trouble leaving him. Some women have children with men they thought they wanted for a lifetime and now they are raising the children alone and the man has moved on.

Slow down.

Be kind to yourself.

Keep your standards in place and be patient—Whatever God pre-destined to occur in your life will happen.

BEGIN AGAIN

"When a person decides to leave you move on—as difficult as it may be."

Men have a way of showing women they are no longer interested. Perhaps there was a series of fights or misunderstandings, which could cause the demise of a relationship. Whatever the reason, people walking out of our lives is hardly ever easy. When a man stops calling or shows a lack of concern when you are speaking, this is a red flag. He is probably preparing to leave you. If he does leave, you must decide to move on. You do not deserve to mourn that relationship forever. Process it, gather yourself, and keep going.

You have a right to be free.

You have a right to continue your life.

You have a right to begin again.

Moving on is not optional, it is necessary.

ALL IS TOO MUCH

"Do not make a man your idol."

I love men just as much as the next woman does. However, I will not make him an idol. When a man wants you to spend all of your time with him (excluding the euphoric early stage of the relationship), that, ladies, is a red flag. Be sure to maintain a healthy balance while building the relationship. Continue to embrace your personal time and the things you enjoy doing.

Do not lose your individuality.

Remember, you are allowed to have space, friends, and free time.

Respecting your man is one thing; making a god out of him is another.

Create healthy boundaries.

9

STANDARDS ARE NONNEGOTIABLE

Everyone's standards are different.

Some people's standards are higher than others.

You create your standards as a model of what you would like dating to look like. They determine how far you will go, how much you will take, and the things you do or do not consent to.

When you meet a man who seeks to override your standards, that is a red flag. Standards (within reason) deserve to be celebrated and not dismantled. It reflects how you feel about yourself.

DO NOT NEGATE
YOUR PURPOSE

*"Remember you were
created with purpose."*

While dating, it is healthy to continue pursuing your dreams, goals, and aspirations. This pursuit will lead you into your purpose. Paying attention to red flags in these areas could mean the difference between your operating in your purpose or not. I have actually been in a position where I allowed a man to consume me.

When I could have been aspiring toward goals, I was waiting by the phone for him to call. At other times, I would allow myself to become so engrossed in him that I did not create space to manage my own personal affairs.

Ladies, make sure you remember that time is precious and something that you cannot get back. Maintain a balance between relationships and actively work toward your purpose. You will thank yourself later.

KNOW YOUR RIGHTS

"Do not allow a relationship to consume you."

Some men can be controlling. They want to know where you are and who you are with at *all* times. They feel as though you being around others is a threat to your relationship. Some men will call and text throughout your entire day in an effort to know your every move. You are not obligated to isolate yourself and respond to all of his inquiries. You are permitted to enjoy your time and space without being interrogated.

You are permitted to enjoy your day, make plans and associate with your friends without being labeled as unloyal. Be careful of entertaining men who carry these attributes. You control your life, not another person.

Do not allow anyone to silence you, monopolize all of your time, or wrap themself so tightly into your life that you feel as though you are being consumed by them. Otherwise, you will lose yourself in the end. Instead, choose freedom. Choose joy. Choose to stand up and enjoy your life. Whether you are dating for leisure or for marriage it deserves to be done from a place of peace and joy, not control.

12

WHILE DATING
REMEMBER
WHO YOU ARE

Women have a habit of losing themselves while dating a man. Why can't we date and remain true to who we are? We absolutely can.

It is imperative that we remain laser-focused on who we are. Yes, we should learn from the men in our lives. Yes, compromise and communication are critical ingredients in a relationship. However, we must not lose ourselves while navigating the "relationship waters."

Your opinions matter.

Your perspective deserves to be heard.

You do not always need to revise the lens you are looking through based on what another person thinks.

BE YOURSELF

"Do not hide who you really are for fear of not being in a relationship."

There is a saying that, when we first meet a person, single people send their representatives. This is often true. There are varied reasons why people do this. Some men are simply deceitful. They may be hiding something that would cause a woman to pause dating them.

In contrast, some women hide who they are for fear of not being in a relationship. If you are a direct person, be direct. If you are a mother, a divorcée, or a minister, do not conceal that information.

Whoever is for you will be able to handle all of you. You will not be viewed as an inconvenience or a burden. Instead, the man that is for you will love the things about you that may cause you to experience internal fear.

14

YOU DESERVE
TO BE SEEN—
NOT HIDDEN

One of the most humiliating moments in my life occurred when the man I thought I loved walked right past my family and me as if we were invisible. I will never forget the pain I felt as I watched him entertain his family while ignoring us.

After leaving that space, I decided I would never entertain anyone else who thought it was okay to hide me. Ladies, your man should be proud to introduce you to his loved ones. An open display of how he feels about you should come naturally. If you are seriously dating, he should invite you out with friends and family. If you are in a committed relationship, you should not be a secret from them.

You are a beautiful creation.

You deserve to be seen and acknowledged.

THE ESSENTIALS

*"Do not jeopardize your peace
and joy to be with someone."*

There are some things money cannot buy. Peace and joy are two of them. You would be amazed to know how many people forfeit their peace and joy to say they are in a relationship.

Is it worth it? Absolutely not.

Make sure you are connecting with men who contribute to a peaceful environment. Watch out for men who are confrontational and argumentative. Does he make you smile, or does he offer up sadness and discouragement? The disruption of peace and joy in your life can lead to internal chaos.

Date with a heightened awareness of what is important to you. Some things cannot be compromised.

AVOID ISOLATION

*"Keep yourself balanced
while dating."*

Do not isolate yourself from friends and family while dating. A healthy family structure consists of security, peace, and strength. These are your people—the ones who know you from the inside out. It is important not to isolate yourself while dating.

Men will always be there.

They are not going anywhere.

It is important to remain connected to your people. Do not allow yourself or a man to drive you away from them. You should include him in your life without separating yourself from those you love.

Allowing a man to isolate you from your loved ones is one of the biggest forms of control. Be careful not to succumb to this.

Be balanced.

A few private moments with your significant other are extremely different from you being restricted from ever gathering with your loved ones.

17

FAMILY & FRIENDS

"Do not allow the inquiries or timelines of family members and friends to pressure you into being with someone."

It can be frustrating when people constantly inquire about your relationship status. I feel that is as private a topic as the medical benefits they receive from their employer.

Do not feel obligated to answer, and do not rush into a relationship because of external pressure.

Take your time.

This is not magic.

You control how you move through relationships. Make sure that you are making decisions for yourself.

18

INTENTIONAL
MONITORING

"When others are getting married, be intentional about monitoring your emotions."

It is easy to desire to be in a relationship when you see so many people in your circle who are dating and or getting married. I recall almost destroying a friendship because I had become jealous of my friend. She was engaged to be married and I was still single. Back then, getting married was what I viewed as the crème de la crème.

My classmates, young adult family members, and now my friends were getting engaged. I transitioned from celebrating my friend to becoming very jealous to the point of no longer being a part of her wedding party. This was one of my worst decisions and it caused an immense amount of distance and frustration between us. I was dead wrong!

I allowed my emotions to overtake me, almost costing me to dismantle a relationship with my childhood friend. I learned that the desire to be in a relationship is natural, but we have to manage our emotions otherwise we can jeopardize the good relationships we have access to. I also learned that expediting relationships can be harmful if it is not organic. Ladies, do not rush into relationships based on what is occurring in the lives of other people.

Try your best not to make someone else's now, determine your next.

You are two different people who are experiencing two different journeys and timelines.

19

GOOD IS NOT
GOOD ENOUGH

*"It is not enough for a man
just to be a good person."*

You must ask yourself if he is good for you.

Relationships are like puzzles—for them to work, the two people must fit with each other. Although some men are genuinely good people, it does not necessarily mean they are a good fit for you.

Be honest with yourself while dating.

Ask yourself if you share the same interests.

Does he hold the same beliefs as you do? Are your views the same as his when it relates to family, politics, and faith?

These are a few of the questions that supersede whether he is a good person.

20

HE LOVES ME—
HE LOVES ME NOT

"You cannot make someone love you."

Trying to force someone to love me was one of the hardest, heart-breaking lessons I have learned. You cannot *make* someone love you. Why would you want to force someone to do what they are not interested in doing?

If he does not love you, he does not love you.

You may cook for him, keep your home tidy, and even encourage him. You can take the "L" in arguments, but he still will not love you. The list of scenarios is endless. I am sharing this with you, ladies, because some of us have a habit of trying to force-feed men into being with us.

You can never make a man do what is not in his heart to do. You must accept it and continue with your life. To ignore these red flags is unnecessarily engaging in self-harm. I want you to be well, not living under the umbrella of shame and disappointment.

When your man finds you, you will not have to force him to do what needs to be done. He will jump at the opportunity to show you how precious you are to him.

21

LOVE IS A DECISION

"'I love you' is an action phrase."

We often hear the words "I love you." Ladies, these words should be accompanied by actions. Love is not goosebumps or the nervous tension you feel in your stomach when you are near a man. Real love is seen through what you do.

Love is not enchantment; it is a decision that we make every day. Through the ups and the downs. Through the good times and bad. We are making decisions to love the other person.

Do not let the words "I love you" solely convince you that a man genuinely loves you. Instead, be observant of the actions that follow.

22

A FALSE REALITY

*"Do not create a mythical
reality to match what you want
your relationship to be."*

On numerous occasions while dating, I was guilty of seeing what I wanted to see, and hearing what I wanted to hear. The problem with that was I created a false idea of my reality. This was dangerous because when the bottom fell out of the relationship, I was left feeling devastated and embarrassed.

When a man is telling you or showing you where he is with you, listen to him! Do not create a false idea of the situation based on what you would like it to be.

Face the facts. Embrace the reality that is yours and move on. The worst thing you can do is ignore what has been said or observed.

23

LET'S BE CLEAR

"Dating and having a sexual partner are two different things."

Let me tell you right here and now that dating and sex are entirely different. Ladies, please take diligent care of yourselves. Just because a man is having sex with you does not mean you two are exclusive or even dating.

Many people regularly have one-night stands. Some of you are still waiting by the phone hoping he will call. Often, he has moved on to his next conquest. Women and men are biologically different.

Women are naturally nurturing. We like to hold on to people and things and nurture them.

Men can detach themselves from people and things significantly more easily than women can.

24

SEX DOES NOT
EQUATE TO LOVE

We often equate sex with love.

This is inaccurate.

Two people can repeatedly have sex without being in love. People have sex for varied reasons. Perhaps it is an addiction. Perhaps it is a way to prevent loneliness. Perhaps it satisfies a natural craving.

Although love is a factor for some, I stress that when you are being intimate with someone, it is not necessarily because they are in love with you.

Protect your mind, body, and spirit.

Remain in conversation.

There is only one you.

25

LOVE IS SIGNIFICANTLY DIFFERENT FROM LUST

Love is loyal.

It reciprocates genuine concern for each other.

It is unselfish.

When someone loves you, they want to know you are well. They are concerned about your peace, goals, safety, and so on.

Lust is different.

It is a heavy, uncontrolled sexual desire.

A person's physique, body language, eyes, smell, or sound can elicit lust. Phrases such as "You look so good" or "You turn me on" flatter some women. They may begin thinking a man loves her because he complimented her. Although good to hear, do not misconstrue compliments as love.

Lust is impulsive—it does not require much responsibility.

26

A MAN KNOWS WHO HE WANTS AND WHO HE DOES NOT WANT

When did it become acceptable to act like men are incompetent?

The truth is they are not.

A man knows who he wants.

I have heard several stories about men who knew they wanted to spend the rest of their lives with women shortly after dating them. In some cases, they knew from the first moment they saw her. Ladies do not pressure men to be a part of your life. If he is not offering what you feel like you deserve, move on.

Do not blow up his phone.

Do not beg and plead.

Do not propose.

Do not feel as though you need to explain your worth. Men are capable of moving through relationships as they choose. If he is showing you that he does not want you, then do not try to force him. You are only hurting yourself. You cannot make people be where they do not want to be. Either you leave or you let them go (whichever comes first).

You must ask yourself why you are fighting for someone who does not want you. If he did concede, would this be the routine you would want to continue for your life? I hope not. Wait for the person who synchronizes with you. A man who enjoys your company, who makes it his priority to please you, include you, and infuse your relationship with joy.

27

DO NOT
COMPROMISE
YOURSELF

Ladies do not compromise yourself or your standards to be with someone. Loving, honoring, and respecting the person that you are with is one thing; compromising yourself is something different. I can recall several times where I went against my own beliefs, my own self-worth and self-respect, in an effort not to be alone.

I remember becoming so desperate to be in this relationship that I tolerated blatant disrespect and repetitive dishonor.

It is not worth it.

Remember who you are.

Remember that you are worthy of respect.

Remember that you are needed and that you are necessary.

Never, ever compromise yourself.

It was too expensive.

Stand up for your principles and values. Understand that the boundaries you have set up in your life protect you. Understand that you have thought this through. You know who you are. You know what you want. You know what your deal breakers are. Do not set that aside because he is framing it as nothing serious. Your values *are* serious.

The way you begin a relationship is the way it will continue.

Compromising yourself and your standards will never work in your favor. Remember that your feelings matter. Your principles and standards are there to protect you.

GENUINE
GENEROSITY

*"A man genuinely interested in
you will be happy to include
you in his spending."*

Some men are naturally generous.

Others, not so much.

It is his prerogative to choose how he spends his money. However, I believe that a man who is interested in you will include you in his spending. It does not have to be thousands of dollars, but it will reflect how sincerely he cares for you. If he only takes you out for fast food and never to a fine-dining restaurant, that could be a red flag.

If you are a legitimate couple and he never celebrates with you, that is a red flag. If you have an emergency and he has the capacity to help but does not, that may be a red flag. Pay attention, ladies. This is not about breaking the bank. It is, however, an indicator that he is really into you.

He should not consider spending money on you or helping you as a burden. It is something he would be proud to do.

CHECKING IN

"If he is unconcerned about your well-being, that is a sign you are insignificant to him."

When a man is genuinely concerned about a woman, she knows. His concern will manifest through acts of kindness such as calling to confirm she arrived at her destination safely, actively listening and engaging in conversations (minor or major) and being accessible when she needs love and care.

Checking in on the one he cares for would not be considered a chore.

Instead, it would be his pleasure to ensure that she is safe, comfortable and supported.

DON'T
UNDERESTIMATE
MEN

"When a man is serious about you,
you will know it."

Ladies, remember that if a man never invites you to dinner or events, or never introduces you to his friends or family, he is not serious about building a future with you. If he never asks you how you are doing or never expresses interest in what is going on in your life, that is a red flag.

Some men will do the bare minimum to keep you around for what they can get from you or what they enjoy about you. Perhaps you have some educational commonalities, or a shared skill set that they may enjoy talking about. Others may be solely physically attracted to you.

It depends.

Every man's needs and desires are different.

At the end of the day, you will know if the relationship is superficial or authentic. Watch for patterns (good or bad) to help you determine whether a man is serious about you.

NO-GO

"He should extend invitations."

If he does not extend an invitation to an event or activity, do not invite yourself. If he excluded you, there is a strong possibility that it was intentional. One of the worst experiences I ever had was when I asked if I could attend a function with my man and his mother. I was so uneducated back then, I actually thought he forgot to invite me. I asked if I could attend, he agreed, and I went. It was the most uncomfortable experience.

They only spoke to me when spoken to. I was unsure what he had told her, so I did not feel free to converse. It was awkward. Ladies, do yourself a favor by not inviting yourself to events or activities. If you are upset (based on the level of your relationship) about not receiving an invitation, discuss it with him and move from there.

If he wants you there, he will invite you.

32

NO MORE CRUMBS

*"Men make time for who
is important to them."*

Women often give men a pass for not spending time with them in the name of not being on the same page or not understanding what women need. What I have learned is that men do exactly what they want to do. They create time for what or who is important to them.

The time for accepting crumbs from the table of men has passed.

Know this.

Men will create time for women who are important to them.

33

BE SMART—
GUARD YOUR
HEART

I have repeatedly witnessed in my personal and shared relationship history where other women and I have not guarded our hearts. Ladies, make sure that you are guarding yourself. There are men out there who are extremely genuine about the kind of woman they are looking for, and they are honest about it during the dating process.

Unfortunately, there are men who are not honest. They will sleep with you while keeping another woman or even women on their side. They are not truthful. They will make fake plans with you about wanting to develop a future with you, but they are actually building it with someone else or just playing around in the streets. So be careful.

Your heart is the biggest part of you.

You deserve transparency.

You deserve protection.

You have to be in charge of your space.

You must advocate for yourself.

INTENTIONAL
INTENSIONS

"If he is not talking about marriage,
it is because he does not want to."

Ladies, if a man is not talking to you about marriage, it is because he does not want to. Stop giving a pass to men who make decisions every day in their lives. You are not an exception to the rule. Just like men function in their career fields and in academia, they have the capacity to function in relationships as well.

You cannot make him marry you. You cannot make him have those conversations. You have to be sure and know that you are worth it. Men make decisions every day for their lives. Do not give a green light or a pass to someone who is intentionally not engaging in conversation about a permanent future with you. Move on. I am not saying that if the conversation arises and he is engaging, you should not engage. I am saying there are some men who are not serious about building a future with you. They are not interested in building a relationship with you. This is why it is good to protect your heart.

Move at a balanced pace.

You must be in his heart.

He must be serious about you.

He must be ready.

He must want you.

Do not be afraid to give him space.

You decide whether you would like to continue with the relationship. If not, you have permission to move on.

35

DECLINE EXCUSES

"Do not make excuses for men."

I believe those who negate accountability give excuses. "I didn't have time." "I forgot." "I was going to do it later." All of these are excuses that cause one not to be accountable for their lack of action. Some men are notorious for giving excuses. Ladies, my hope for you is that you take loving care of yourselves. A man who makes excuses, is a man who is not prepared to take your relationship to the next level.

He is not ready to commit to paying the cost of what it would take to be in a solid relationship with you.

No more excuses.

Stop letting men off the hook because they repeatedly give you a line. You are more intelligent and savvier than that. You are worth more than that. Treat yourself like you deserve to be treated. Know that you are worth the commitment, worth the dedication, worth the loyalty.

You are worth being with someone who performs at an acceptable level.

36

STAY IN YOUR LANE

*"It is not your job to convince
a man to marry you."*

It is not your job, ladies, to convince a man to marry you. Live your life. Pay attention to what you see and to what you hear. Listen with your heart, not just with your ears. No amount of groveling, begging, pleading, explaining, or giving visual aids will make a man commit to you for life.

A man who is ready to commit to you, to marry you, to make you his wife, to build together, will let you know through his actions, his support, and his loyalty. Do not pressure him to commit to you. Let him go. If he is for you, he will return to you as the best version of himself.

You deserve to be with someone who wants to be with you. You are worth it.

SPEAK UP

"Unaddressed disrespect will continue."

I passionately believe that people do what you allow them to do. Do not tolerate disrespect. Men have the capacity to be warm, welcoming, respectful, and kind. That is what you should require. Anything less means that we are not compatible. That is definitely a deal-breaker for me.

Determine what is not okay and stand up for yourself. Address disrespect when it occurs. In some instances, a conversation may suffice. In other instances, discarding the relationship will be the only option.

Pay close attention to that red flag. Acknowledging it could save you. Ignoring it has the potential to break you.

38

FAILED RELATIONSHIPS CALL FOR ACCOUNTABILITY

If the relationship fails, you must take ownership for the role you played, even if that role includes ignoring visible signs, better known as red flags. On the outside looking in, it feels so good to blame everyone else for our failed relationships. The truth of the matter is, there is a role that we play in that failure as well, even if it means we failed ourselves by ignoring the red flags.

There comes a time when we must take responsibility for our carelessness in the relationship. It cannot always be the other person's fault. Perhaps we could have spoken differently or done things differently. Relationships fail for a myriad of reasons.

I want to encourage you, though, ladies, to take a deep look within and see what your part was, own it, do not repeat it and move forward.

39

FAMILIARITY
CAN BREED
RED FLAGS

When you see another woman roaming through your man's home (especially his bedroom), that normally means they are together. I once ignored red flags when a woman who was frequently around the man I was dating—washing his dishes, freely entering his bedroom and going to events with him. If a woman seems that familiar with your guy, it usually means he has allowed a serious level of intimacy to occur.

Back then, I was committed to the idea that we would be together (despite all the red flags). Epic mistake! Her familiarity with him and his space was as if she was in a relationship with him. "If a woman seems too familiar with your guy, it's possibly an indication that he's opened the door of intimacy with her." I recall feeling as though I was over-thinking their relationship, turns out my assumptions were accurate. They were a couple, too.

40

DO NOT BE
DECEIVED

Do not fall for the "you're just overreacting or being insecure" line. If you were not an insecure person prior to meeting him, then chances are it is your female intuition warning you that something is not right.

One of the most vivid memories of one of my failed relationships was when I confronted my guy about how I felt about his being in the presence of so many different women. He always countered that I was overreacting, I was not seeing clearly, I was misunderstanding or misinterpreting the relationship.

Ladies, pay attention. When men accuse you of misinterpreting what you know you clearly see and hear, that is a red flag. Please do yourself a favor—do not ignore it. Do not ignore the conversations, the late-night phone calls, the sneaking around, and the women's signatures for intimate items.

You are an intellectual.

Do not diminish your faculties based on the convincing lies that some men may tell. You know what you feel. Pay attention to that.

41

EYES WIDE OPEN

I want you to keep your eyes wide open. When red flags appear, do not ignore them. I remember being at home and receiving a text from my man. It was an image of him, our newborn baby, and another woman at an event! My heart dropped into my stomach. I could not believe it. When I confronted him, he said, "Oh, it was just a game. Her daughter works with the team." The fact is, if it was innocent, why not get me a ticket, too? Why would he send me that picture? Red flags were waving all around me. He was trying to get me to leave the relationship, and I was too blind to see it. I knew I had been disrespected. I knew I did not trust him, but I continued trying to make us work.

Ladies do not ignore what is directly in front of you. Choose respect. Choose peace. Choose to honor yourself even when others do not. Keep your eyes wide open, be courageous, and take the appropriate steps necessary for you to open yourself to new relationships (if that is what you want) where the man will honor and respect you.

42

TAKE TIME
TO PROCESS

When someone has hurt you and the truth has become known, do not allow them to rush you through your process. Take your time. I vividly recall being in a relationship, and it fell apart. The person I was seeing secretly married someone else while he was still dating me. He "accidentally" left his wedding ring on. He came to my home, I mentioned the ring and he gave an excuse that it was just a gift from his female friend and her family. I was done! I then discovered that they had gotten married. Shortly after his secret was revealed, he began rushing me to get past the hurt.

Do not allow anyone to rush you through your process, whether you found out the honest way because he confessed or you found out accidentally. You deserve time to process and release all your feelings.

Remember, no one has the right to control your reaction to tough news. Take care of yourself. Take your time to deal with the reality of what has occurred. It is not anyone's place to rush you through your process.

Take your time to heal.

TRUSTED VOICES

"Listen to the trusted voices in your life."

Listen to the trusted voices in your life. When I was growing up, as a teenager and as a young woman, I learned that it was okay to listen to older adults and those more experienced than I was to avoid danger. I encourage you to listen to those who you believe have your best interest at heart.

Do not ignore those full of wisdom, who have walked that road, who have had difficulties, struggles, and victories. Listen to what they have to say. Now, I want to be clear, I am not talking about everybody, but there is someone that God has placed in your life you can trust, who has experience beyond your level of experience, who may have years on you, who has a voice and track record that could help you navigate your relationship.

Listen to them.

It will benefit you.

There are times when your age should not take precedence over the experience of those who have gone before you.

Be open to helpful feedback.

Actively listening to good advice could potentially save you from missteps and even heartbreak.

REMAIN TRUE
TO YOURSELF

I want to encourage you to remain true to yourself. Unfortunately, there are people who are extremely insecure, and they would like to project that insecurity onto you. Be who you are. If you are educated, be that. If you have a phenomenal career, walk in that.

You do not have to dumb down yourself to be in a relationship. Whoever is for you will honor that part of you, fully respect you, and be proud to go through life with you.

45

LET YOURSELF
OFF THE HOOK

Do not be quick to subscribe to the idea that you are not in a relationship because there is something wrong with you. Know who *you* are. This is important because outsiders do not know the intricate details of who you are or your heart's desires. Ladies, I want you to let yourself off the hook. There is nothing wrong with you.

Unfortunately, people feel that it is okay to comment on your status if you are a single woman. They feel it is okay to ask you randomly, "Where's your guy?" "Why are you still alone?" "Why are you not married? Why have you never been married?" Some have the nerve to say there must be something wrong with you. That is incorrect.

Everyone, whether single or married, needs enhancement. So no, that is not always the reason you are single. That mindset is a red flag. Sometimes you are single because you are still growing. Sometimes it is because you have not met the right person yet. And sometimes, it is simply because marriage is not your goal— and that is perfectly okay.

There is nothing wrong with you.

RESPECT

"You must require respect."

Respect means considering someone as worthy of high regard. Ladies, I want to remind you that it is important that you require respect while dating. It is not okay for men to speak to you disrespectfully. It is not okay for them to put their hands on you. It is not okay for them to ignore you or not spend time with you. You must require respect.

Now, you cannot make a man do anything. But when he disrespects you, address it immediately. If he acts cavalier or as though he has done nothing wrong, that's a red flag. Men who see no issue with their behavior are guaranteed to repeat it. Remember, you are a woman who is worthy of respect. Do not allow men to treat or speak to you in a degrading manner. Do not allow them to treat your body as if it is not precious. You must speak out against disrespect. If disrespect continues you will need to make the decision to exit the relationship.

It is imperative that you know what you deserve. Do not defend disrespectful behavior. It is unacceptable. Perhaps the man you are dating came from a broken home or was raised in a toxic environment. You are not the "fixer." Allow him to seek professional help or counsel elsewhere. Dating a man who disrespects you will most likely expose you to some of his toxic traits. Honestly, it has the potential to become an unsafe environment for you.

47

YOU ARE
VALUABLE

It is imperative that you remember that you are valuable. The difference between a used car dealership and a luxury car dealership is that the cheaper cars lead with their prices. When you see a commercial for a luxury vehicle, you will note that its price is not the focus because its quality speaks for itself. Also, the amount of the vehicle does not intimidate those who can afford it. They are interested in the car's longevity, its interior comfort and its advanced technology.

You need to remember that you are valuable, a woman of exceptional quality. Understand that you are priceless, special, and unique. A real man will identify you as invaluable and treat you as such. Knowing that you are priceless places you in a different category. You will wear pride like a garment and confidence will precede you.

Recognizing these qualities about yourself will release you to be selective without guilt or restraint. Men will also notice these beautiful qualities in you, setting you up for more favorable introductions and or relationships.

This is not arrogance.

It is however the doorway that will escort you to better relationship opportunities.

48

EMBRACE YOUR
WOMAN'S
INTUITION

I want to encourage you to embrace your woman's intuition. It is a special gift to be able to rely on your quick and ready insight. That is your discernment. That is your spirit letting you know that something is off, right, wrong or missing. Your woman's intuition alerts you that something needs to be discussed, dropped or managed. Your woman's intuition is to be taken seriously. It is a gift that will either save you much grief and heartache or offer increased opportunities for joy, and happiness. Pay attention to your woman's intuition. To ignore it could be costly.

Your woman's intuition exceeds basic logic. It alerts you internally. It is your God-given instinct. My mom used to encourage us to follow our first mind, that's your woman's intuition. Your intuition manifests when acts of faith or leaps should be taken but they also manifest when red flags appear.

WITH OR
WITHOUT YOU

I have much respect for men, especially those who are honest about their intentions. Unfortunately some men are not open about where they are emotionally and what they really want. Ladies, allow me to encourage you to remain hopeful. Do not allow the immaturity of others to discourage you from "getting out there." On the other hand, if you've decided a relationship is not what you desire, go after the dream that you are passionate about.

Be sure your decision-making is based on what you want. Do not give anyone else power over you to control what your next steps are. Ladies, do not allow failed relationships from the past or the present to disqualify you from having the exceptional future that awaits you.

50

**THE SOONER
THE BETTER**

The sooner you recognize red flags, the better. Recognizing them early in a relationship will open doors for you to have more time to connect to the person you are supposed to be with and build with. If you can identify your deal-breakers when you meet a person, then you will have saved time.

The longer you entertain people who throw up red flags, the less time you have to connect with a person who is right for you. My prayer for you is that you denounce toxic relationships, acknowledge red flags in the behavior of others, and be open to receiving that person who is right for you.

You deserve the absolute best!

P.O. Box 453
Powder Springs, Georgia 30127
www.entegritypublishing.com
info@entegritypublishing.com